Marmite Cookbook

Luscious and Scrumptious Marmite Recipes

BY

Christina Tosch

Copyright Notes

Table of Contents

Introduction

There are hundreds of ways to use this luscious and flavorful food spread. The basic and traditional method is to spread it over toast and place a few layers of different types of cheese over it and serve. But now, several other ways have been introduced to use this food spread, marmite, and make various amazingly luscious recipes for yourself or friends or family. This is something that goes well with any recipe you make.

There are 30 delicious recipes in this cookbook that you must try if you love marmites like dippy egg and marmite soldiers, marmite pork ribs, marmite beef stew, marmite pasta, marmite spaghetti, marmite and French onion soup, marmite and carrot soup, and many more. So, as you can see, few recipes are for breakfast, a few are for lunch or dinner, or a few of them are even soups. You can also experiment with different types of food you make, try including marmite as one of the ingredients and you will see how magical marmite is!

1. Marmite Roasted Onions

Onions are mostly used as one of the basic ingredients in our food and there are very few chances where we use them as the main ingredients in our recipes, right! This is one such recipe where onions are the main ingredient, Marmite Roasted Onions. This recipe is quite new for so many people, you might have not heard of it but trust me, it is an amazing recipe which you can make within a few minutes. To make this recipe, you just need three ingredients: onions then, butter, and of course, star, marmite. Do try this fun and crispy recipe right away!

Ingredients:

- 4 medium onions (peeled)
- 3/8 cups of butter (unsalted)
- 2 tbsp of marmite

Cooking Time - 1 hour 5 minutes

Serving Size - 4

Instructions:

Preheat the oven at 200°C.

Meanwhile, melt the butter in a saucepan over a low flame.

Now, cut down the onions into two halves, do not remove the stalk, and take out a little part from both of its ends.

Take a baking dish and place the onions over it, pour the marmite as well as butter over the onions.

Then, cover them with foil paper and keep them in the oven.

Let them bake for about 45 minutes, take off the foil paper and again let them bake for another 20 minutes.

Serve them immediately.

2. Dippy Egg and Marmite Soldiers

It is quite fun to make this recipe, as you can see in the picture given below here. The name and the recipe are both quite fascinating, right! But you might now be thinking that it would be really difficult to make it as we''. But that is not the case, you will require only four ingredients over here as eggs, bread, butter, and yes, marmite. Take out just 10 minutes in the morning out of your busy, tight schedule, and have this delicious yet healthy breakfast.

Ingredients:

- 2 eggs
- 4 slices of white bread
- 1 stick of butter
- 2 tbsp marmite
- Seeds (for garnishing)

Cooking Time - 10 minutes

Serving Size - 2

Instructions:

Boil the water first in a pot and once it starts to boil, add eggs into it.

Turn the flame to simmer and keep them as it is for about 2 minutes. Make sure to cover the pot.

Meanwhile, take the slices of bread and toast them with the help of a toaster.

Apply the first thin layer of butter on the bread and then, apply one thinner layer of marmite.

Cut the shapes of soldiers out of the slices of bread. Press them into the egg.

Garnish with the seeds.

Serve immediately!

3. Marmite Chicken

It is always so fun to try new and innovative recipes of chicken every time, is that the same case with you as well? This recipe is a very delicious and mouth-watering one, you must try this one. You have to marinate the chicken pieces first, then prepare the marmite sauce, and mix with the fried chicken cubes. You are salivating, right! The chicken is quite juicy and spicy and delicious due to the strong flavor of marmite and you are going to love this flavor for sure. Try it once and you will fall in love with it!

Ingredients:

- 12 oz. of chicken thigh (cubed, boneless)
- 2 oz. of cornstarch
- 1/4 tsp of baking soda
- 1 egg white
- Cooking oil (deep frying)

For the marinade

- 1/4 tsp soy sauce
- 1/4 tsp of white pepper
- 2 tsp of cornstarch
- 1 tbsp of rice wine
- 1 tbsp of cooking oil

For the marmite mixture

- 2 tsp of Marmite
- 2 tsp of light soya sauce
- 1-1/2 tsp of honey
- 1-1/2 tsp of maltose
- 1 tsp of sesame oil
- 3 tbsp of water

Cooking Time - 15 minutes

Serving Size - 4

Instructions:

Take a bowl and mix soya sauce, white pepper, cornstarch, rice wine, and cooking oil.

Marinate the chicken pieces with the above marinade for about 30 minutes.

Now, take another bowl and mix cornstarch with baking soda.

Then, take the marinated chicken and coat it with egg white first and then with the mixture of cornstarch as well as baking soda.

Deep fry the pieces of chicken and once they are fried, keep them on the paper towel to remove excess oil out of them.

Now, place a pan over medium flame and add marmite, light soya sauce, honey, maltose, sesame oil, and water into it. Stir it.

Add the chicken into the marmite mixture and stir gently.

Turn off the flame and serve!

4. Marmite Pork Ribs

If you are planning for a get-together or a family dinner or planning to call your friends for a party, this will help you. This recipe of marmite pork ribs is perfect for such occasions as these are super luscious, and the best thing is that you can prepare these within 25 minutes. This goes well with a glass of chilled beer. You just need to marinate the pork, double fry it and then make a mixture of marmite with honey and mix them. Finally, season it and serve!

Ingredients:

- Marinade of Pork ribs
- 12 pieces of pork
- 1 tbsp of soy sauce
- 1 tbsp of hao xing wine
- Pepper (seasoning)
- 5 tbsp cornstarch
- 2 tbsp sauce
- 1 tsp of marmite
- 3 tbsp of honey
- 1 tsp of soy sauce
- 1 tbsp of Worcestershire sauce
- 3 cloves of garlic
- 1 shallot
- Oil
- Sesame seeds (toasted)

Cooking Time - 25 minutes

Serving Size - 3

Instructions:

Add pork ribs, marinade, soy sauce, and hao xing wine into a zip-lock bag. Mix them quite well.

Marinade the pork ribs for an hour in the refrigerator within a zip-lock bag.

Take a pan and place it over a high flame.

Add oil into it for frying the marinated pork ribs.

Once they are fried well, apply or coat them with the cornstarch and once again fry them. Adjust the flame according to you here.

Once you have double fried the pork ribs, take a bowl and mix honey with the marmite, add a few drops of water as well.

Now, take another pan and add a little bit of oil into it.

Once the oil is heated up, add garlic as well as shallots into it.

Stir them for a minute and then, add a mixing sauce of vegemite and honey.

Mix them with the seasoning and Worcestershire sauce. Stir them and finally add fried pork to this mixture.

Serve hot!

5. Marmite and Mustard Savoury Biscuits

This recipe of marmite and mustard savoury biscuits will help to get rid of sugary biscuits that might have gotten you addicted. These biscuits are savory in taste, crispy, crumbly as well as crunchy in texture and taste amazing. If you are looking for something healthy as well as delicious as your appetizer, then this can be the perfect choice in that case. Prepare them and store them in an air-tight container for the next few days!

Ingredients:

- 1/4 cup of Stork margarine
- 1/2 tbsp of mustard
- 1 tsp of flakes of yeast
- 1 tsp of Marmite
- 1/2 plain flour
- 2 tbsp of water

Cooking Time - 30 minutes

Serving Size - 1

Instructions:

Preheat the oven at 200°C.

Take a bowl and mix mustard with marmite, stork margarine, and yeast flakes as well.

Now, add the flour into the above-prepared mixture and mix them well with the help of your hands.

Now, form the dough out of it by gradually adding water into it.

Knead it well to make a soft dough. Make the shapes of sausages with it.

Then, keep them in the refrigerator for about 20 minutes.

Once they are chilled, cut them into small pieces and let them bake for about 15 minutes.

Serve hot!

6. Cheesy Marmite Crumpet Bake

This recipe of cheesy marmite crumpet bake is ready to be your next favorite snack or appetizer. This is a crunchy, crumbly, and super delicious recipe you can ever make for yourself. This might seem quite difficult to make, but honestly, it is not. You can make this recipe in just 20 minutes, try this recipe on weekends for your kids and family, they are going to love them for sure. These baked crumpets can be best paired with a hot cup of tea or coffee as your evening snacks. You must try this right away!

Ingredients:

- 6 pieces of crumpets
- Butter as needed
- 2 tbsp marmite
- 1 cup of cheese (grated)
- 4 eggs
- 2-3 tbsp of Milk
- Salt
- Pepper

Cooking Time - 20 minutes

Serving Size - 2

Instructions:

Initially, toast the crumpets, apply a thin layer of butter over them, and then apply a marmite layer.

Now, cut all the crumpets into two halves and place them all on the baking dish.

Take a bowl and whisk the eggs into it, add a little bit of milk into it. Season it with salt and pepper according to your taste.

Then, sprinkle some of the grated cheese over the crumpets and then, drizzle the egg mixture over them as well.

Then, sprinkle some more cheese over them.

Let them bake at 180°C for about 20 minutes.

Serve immediately!

7. Cheese and Marmite Toastie

Cheese and marmite toasts are rich as well as savory in taste, cheesy, and super yummy. This is very easy to make and you just need four ingredients like bread, butter, marmite, of course, and cheese, and you are done in just 10 minutes. You can prepare a satisfying and yummy brekkie and pair it with a cup of hot tea or coffee. This makes a perfect breakfast for your kids or you can just pack these for the lunch box for your kids who want new things all the time. This is surely a change for them.

Ingredients:

- 2 slices of white or brown bread
- 1 tbsp of butter
- 1/2 tsp of Marmite
- 1/4 cup of cheese (shredded)

Cooking Time - 10 minutes

Serving Size - 1

Instructions:

Apply a thin layer of butter over the surface of the bread and then apply another thin layer of marmite as well.

Now, sprinkle the cheese over the bread and let them toast in the toaster oven.

Then, finally, serve it either in a sandwich form or serve them as open-faced.

8. Marmite Avocado Toast

Marmite is something that you can add to any of your food, it goes just perfect with any of the recipes. This recipe is quite simple to make, all you need to do is sauté the mushroom, toast bread, apply a marmite layer on the slice of the bread, then another layer of the mashed avocados, and keep the cooked mushrooms over it. Then, serve. See, it's that easy and quick, you just need ten minutes to have these amazing marmite avocado toasts. Give it a try and you will never *be* going to turn around.

Ingredients:

- 1 tsp of Olive oil
- 8 oz. of button mushrooms
- 4 slices of white bread
- 1 avocado (ripened, mashed)
- 1 tbsp of Marmite
- Salt
- Pepper
- Chili flakes

Cooking Time - 10 minutes

Serving Size - 2

Instructions:

Place a saucepan over a medium flame and heat olive oil into it.

Take a damp towel and rub the mushrooms with it and remove the dirt from them.

Chop the mushrooms. Keep them in the saucepan in a single layer and let them cook until they get brown from one side. Flip them all and cook them from another side as well.

Now, season them with salt, pepper, and chili flakes.

Meanwhile, toast the slices of bread.

Then, apply a layer of marmite on every slice of the bread.

Then, apply one thicker layer of mashed avocado.

Finally, garnish them with cooked mushrooms and then season with more chili flakes as well as black pepper.

Serve and enjoy!

9. Cheese and Marmite Scones

Are you craving something tasty, crunchy, and savory? You have got a perfect recipe here, yes, cheese and marmite scones are here for satisfying your cravings. These cute little crunchy, as well as crumbly balls, are going to be your next favorite afternoon appetizer. You can make these in advance and store them as well for the next 4-5 days. Just give it a try and you will love it for sure.

Ingredients:

- 3-5/8 cups of all-purpose flour + a little more for dusting
- 1 tbsp of baking powder
- 3 tsp of Marmite
- 1 large egg
- 1 cup of milk
- 1 tbsp of sunflower oil
- 1/2 cup of cheddar cheese (grated)
- 1/4 cup of cream cheese

Cooking Time - 15 minutes

Serving Size - 8

Instructions:

Preheat the oven at 220°C. Take a baking sheet and dust it a little with the flour.

Take a bowl and mix baking powder with the flour.

Then, take a jug and add egg, a teaspoon of marmite, and fill the jug with the milk until the overall quantity becomes 300 ml. Mix it well to dissolve the marmite properly.

Take a bowl and mix more than half of the cheddar cheese with the cream cheese as well as the rest of the marmite. Your spread is ready.

Now, add the rest of the cheese to the flour mixture as well as add the milk mixture. Mix them all and form a dough.

Take the dough out of the bowl and knead it on the lightly dusted surface with the flour.

Now, lightly roll the dough and form a long cylinder of it. Cut out 8 pieces from it and shape them into flat rounds.

Keep them all on the baking sheet. Let them bake for about 15 minutes.

Let them cool on the wire rack.

Serve and enjoy!

10. Marmite and Lentil Soup

Soups are one of the best meals in winters, especially when it is snowing, right? This marmite and lentil soup are some of the perfect soups you can have on super cold nights in winter. This soup has rich, savory, and spicy (not too much) flavor to make you beg for it more and more. This soup is not only delicious and palatable but healthy as it has potatoes, mushrooms, lentils, celery, vegetable stock, and many more. You must try this soup, you will love it!

Ingredients:

- 2 tbsp of olive oil
- 1 onion (chopped)
- 1 tsp of garlic (crushed)
- 1 tsp of ginger (grated)
- 2 potatoes (diced)
- 1 tsp of coriander (grounded)
- 1 tsp of cumin (grounded)
- 3-1/2 oz. of button mushrooms (sliced)
- 2 stalks of celery (sliced)
- 2-1/4 cups of brown lentils
- 1 tbsp of Marmite
- 1 tbsp of lemon juice
- 2 cups of vegetable stock
- Greek yogurt (for serving)
- Chives (for serving)
- Crunchy bread (for serving)

Cooking Time - 20 minutes

Serving Size - 4

Instructions:

Place a frypan over a medium flame and heat olive oil into it.

Sauté garlic as well as ginger for about 3 minutes. Then, stir potatoes and let them cook until they become soft.

Then, add cumin, celery, coriander, and mushrooms. Let them cook for about 3 minutes.

Stir lentils and season with lemon juice as well as marmite.

Finally, add the vegetable stock into the frypan and turn down the flame to simmer, and let it cook for 20 minutes.

Serve them in the bowls, top with a little bit of yogurt, bread, and chives.

11. Garlic Marmite Honey Pork Belly

This particular recipe of garlic marmite honey pork belly is way more popular than you have ever heard of. This is very easy to make, simple, as well as it tastes amazing that you will lick all your fingers and will beg for more of it. This recipe is quite classy and wonderful as well. This is perfect for your family dinner and the best part is that you just need 15 minutes to make this, isn't it amazing! Just try it once, you will fall in love with this recipe.

Ingredients:

- 2 lb. of pork belly (small pieces)

For the Marinade

- 1/3 tbsp of salt + chicken seasoning + pepper
- 1 large egg
- 3 tsp of corn flour
- 1 tsp of marmite
- 1/3 tbsp of soy sauce

For the cooking

- 4 cloves of garlic
- 3 tsp of vegetable oil
- 3 tsp of marmite
- 1 tbsp of soy sauce
- 6 tsp of honey
- 1-1/2 cup of stock
- Salt to taste
- 2 tbsp of honey
- 3 tsp of Oyster sauce
- 1 tsp of dark soy sauce
- Rest of the marinade
- Sesame seed (for garnishing)

Cooking Time - 15 minutes

Serving Size - 3

Instructions:

Take a bowl, mix corn flour, marmite, salt, pepper, chicken seasoning, egg, and soy sauce.

Now, add pork pieces into it, mix well and keep it aside for about 2 hours.

Now, take another bowl and mix stock, honey, dark soy sauce, marmite, sugar, oyster sauce, salt, and soya sauce. Place the rest of the marinade to use it next time.

Then, heat the oil in a saucepan and cook pork for about 7 minutes. Turn off the flame and let them cool down a bit.

Take a pan, add cooking oil, heat it through, and stir garlic for about 2-3 minutes.

Pour the sauce as well as the rest of the marinade mixture into the pan. Let it boil for about 5 minutes.

Finally, add pork into it, stir well, coat the pork with the sauce properly.

Sprinkle the sesame seeds over it to garnish.

Serve hot!

12. Marmite Spaghetti

Pasta is something which you can anytime, anywhere, and no matter how many times. This is a very unique as well as a classic version of what normal pasta you eat, this Italian recipe will make you head over heels for this. In this recipe, you will need spaghetti, a few veggies like mushrooms, now you can choose any variety of mushrooms you like. Here we have used button mushrooms, parsley, lots and lots of parmesan cheese, marmite, and seasonings. Just take 10 minutes out of your busy schedules and make it.

Ingredients:

- of Spaghetti
- 5oz. of button Mushrooms (sliced)
- 1/4 cup of Parmesan (grated)
- 2 tbsp of Butter (Unsalted, melted)
- 2 tsp of Marmite
- 1 clove of garlic (minced)
- 1 tbsp of Parsley (minced)
- Salt
- Black Pepper
- Olive Oil (for frying)
- Parmesan (for garnishing)

Cooking Time - 10 minutes

Serving Size - 2

Instructions:

Boil the water and add spaghetti into it, until tender.

Meanwhile, place a pan over a medium flame and heat oil through. Add mushrooms and fry them until they turn brown.

Now, add garlic with salt as well as pepper and let them cook for another 2 minutes.

Add butter and 1/3 cup of the pasta water. Stir well and turn down the flame and add marmite.

Once it gets a little thickened, add spaghetti, toss them well.

Finally, sprinkle parsley as well as parmesan. Once the sauce gets the appropriate thickness, turn off the flame.

Serve hot!

13. Marmite Beef Stew

This classic recipe of marmite beef stew is amazing to have on a cold winter night. This beef stew has one more additional flavor of yeast extract that makes it even tastier as well as delicious. In this recipe, we have used carrots and tomatoes, if you want, you can exchange a few other veggies as well. This requires a little bit more time to cook it but it is all worth it. It is a must-try recipe.

Ingredients:

- 3 tbsp of cooking oil
- 2-1/2 lbs. of chuck roast (bite-sized)
- 2 stalks of celery (sliced)
- 1 onion (chopped)
- 2 carrots (bite-sized)
- 3 cloves of garlic (minced)
- 3 tbsp of Marmite
- 14-1/2 oz. of tomatoes (diced)
- 2 cups of water
- Salt
- 1/4 tsp of pepper
- 4 potatoes (cubed)

Cooking Time - 2 hours 5 minutes

Serving Size - 8

Instructions:

Take a Dutch oven and add cooking oil, heat it through.

Add half of the beef into the oven and cook for about 7 minutes.

Take it out and repeat the same procedure to the rest of the beef. Take this out as well.

Now, add onion, carrot, and celery to the oven and sauté it for 3 minutes.

Then, add garlic as well and sauté for half a minute.

Finally, add the cooked beef again to the oven. Add marmite, water, and cover it with the lid and let it boil.

Reduce the flame to low for 1-1/2 hours.

Add potato, pepper, and salt to it, stir, and cook for another 15 minutes.

Turn off the flame and serve hot!

14. Marmite Sweet Potato Chips

Chips are perfect for your snack time, right, you can pair them with your tea or coffee. You don't need to purchase them every time from the market, you can make them by yourself at home. Yes, you read it correctly, you will need only four ingredients for this: apple cider, vinegar, marmite, sweet potatoes, and a little bit of water. This is a very simple recipe and you will get your crunchy, crispy, and a little spicy chip within half an hour. You can make them in advance, make them, and store them in an air-tight container, or serve them with ketchup or any of your favorite sauce!

Ingredients:

- 4 sweet potatoes (sliced - 1/8")
- 1/2 cup of hot water
- 2 tbsp of marmite
- 2 tbsp of apple cider vinegar

Cooking Time - 35 minutes

Serving Size - 4

Instructions:

Keep the sliced sweet potatoes aside in a bowl.

Take a blender and add water, marmite, and vinegar. Blend it at high speed for 2 minutes and it will become foamy.

Pour this mixture into the bowl of sweet potatoes and toss it well with the help of your hands.

Keep the bowl aside for about 15 minutes.

Heat the oven to 400°F.

Take a baking sheet and keep all the slices of sweet potatoes as a single layer on it.

Let them bake for about 35 minutes.

Serve!

15. Cheesy Marmite Straws

Kids always want something new for their snack time, you agree right! This can be the next appetizer for them. These cheesy, crispy, and crunchy marmites twisted straws are quite easy to make and you just need 15 minutes for this. Four ingredients are required here as marmite, puff pastry, cheese, and egg wash, this is super-duper easy, just make them and have fun!

Ingredients:

- 3 Puff Pastry
- 2 tbsp marmite
- 1/2 cup of Cheese (Grated)
- Egg Wash

Cooking Time - 15 minutes

Serving Size - 15 sticks

Instructions:

Make an oblong with puff pastry.

Apply the marmite over a half part of the puff pastry and then sprinkle some cheese over it.

Now, fold the pastry to enclose marmite and cheese.

Cut them into long sticks then, twist a little bit, and keep them on the baking sheet as a single layer.

Brush them with the egg wash. Let them bake at 190°F for 15 minutes.

Let them cool down a bit and serve!

16. Marmite Pasta

This Italian pasta is everyone's all-time favorite recipe and in this particular recipe, we have enhanced its flavor by adding marmite into it. This cheesy, flavorful, and buttery recipe of pasta will be your perfect breakfast, appetizer, or lunch when you actually do not want to make anything. Just try this recipe once, as it is super easy to make and all you need is just 10 minutes and with just four ingredients, isn't it amazing! It is right, then try it right away!

Ingredients:

- 7 oz. of Pasta
- A knob of Butter
- 2 tbsp of Marmite
- 1/4 cup of cheese (grated)

Cooking Time - 10 minutes

Serving Size - 2

Instructions:

Take a saucepan and cook pasta according to the instructions given on the package.

Once the pasta is cooked, drain the water, and reduce the flame to low, and keep the pasta in the saucepan again.

Now, add butter and half of the cheese into it. Stir it well.

Finally, add marmite, toss them well and let the pasta cook for about 7 minutes while stirring it.

Garnish it with the rest of the cheese and Serve!

17. Cucumber, Marmite, And Cream Sandwich

For any type of party, we have a particular section of different varieties of sandwiches, is that the same case with you as well? If not, then, what are you thinking of? You can add this particular variety to one of the other types of sandwiches. For this recipe, the ingredients are very common, which you can find easily in your kitchen and they are cucumber, slices of bread, marmite, chives, mint leaves, cheese, and butter. Just try this recipe and you will always keep this for your summer party.

Ingredients:

- 1/3 cup of cheese (soft and light)
- 2 tbsp of mint leaves (chopped)
- 1 tbsp of chives (chopped)
- 6 slices of white bread
- 1/2 cucumber (sliced)
- Black pepper powder
- Butter (softened)
- Marmite (to spread)

Cooking Time - 10 minutes

Serving Size - 12

Instructions:

Take a bowl and mix cheese, chives, and mint leaves with black pepper powder as seasoning.

Spread the above paste on 3 bread slices.

Then, make a layer of cucumber slices over them.

Now, take other slices of bread and apply a layer of butter and a layer of marmite over it.

Finally, sandwich both types of slices together and eradicate the crust portion of them.

Cut each sandwich into four slices.

Serve immediately!

18. Marmite Veg Burger

Burgers are one of the most common fast foods you would ever see. It is not limited to any one country; it is appreciated by people all around the world. People from different countries made their versions of burgers now. So, likewise, we have one more type of burger that we have brought for you. This recipe of marmite veg burger is super delicious and yummy that you are sure to beg for more.

This is quite easy to prepare and within just 15 minutes. Give it a try, guys!

Ingredients:

- 1 tbsp of olive oil
- 1 cup of portobello mushrooms (chopped)
- 1/2 onion (chopped)
- 2 cloves of garlic (crushed)
- 1 tbsp of tomato paste
- 2 tsp of marmite
- 1 tsp of cumin (grounded)
- 1 tsp of paprika (smoked)
- 2 cups can black beans (rinsed and drained)
- 1-1/4 cup of brown rice (cooked)
- 1 cup of rolled oats
- 1 egg

For Serving

- 6 whole-grain buns
- 3 tbsp of mayonnaise
- 1/2 onion (sliced)
- 2 tomatoes (sliced)
- 1/3 cup of lettuce

Cooking Time - 15 minutes

Serving Size - 6

Instructions:

Place a frypan over medium flame and heat 1/2 tbsp of olive oil. Add onions, garlic, and mushrooms into the saucepan.

Let them cook for about 5 minutes until they get tender.

Now, add Marmite, paprika, tomato paste, and cumin into it, and let them cook for another 2-3 minutes.

Turn off the flame.

Take a food processor and add the mixture of mushrooms, rice, beans, pepper, egg, and oats into it.

Blend them well and then, take it out and form 6 patties out of this.

Take a frypan once again and heat the rest of the olive into it at medium flame.

Cook all the 6 patties from both sides and for about 3 minutes each.

Cut the buns into two halves and place mayo, patty, onion, lettuce, tomato, and finally, top it with another half of the bun.

Serve and enjoy!

19. Marmite Chickpeas

If you are on a diet and looking for some delicious and spicy snacks, your search is complete here. These crunchy, crispy, and palatable marmite chickpeas are your answer. This recipe is so damn easy to prepare and for this, you will need only two ingredients: chickpeas, and the lead ingredient, marmite. You just have to roast them once and then coat them with marmite, and again roast them. See, it is all done!

Ingredients:

- 2 cups of chickpeas (drained, rinsed)
- 1 tsp of Marmite

Cooking Time - 40 minutes

Serving Size - 2

Instructions:

Preheat the oven at 350°F.

Keep the rinsed chickpeas on the paper towel and let them dry well.

Once they are dried well, place them on the baking sheet arranged with parchment paper.

Let them roast for about 10 minutes.

Transfer them into a bowl and stir them with marmite, coating them well.

Place all the chickpeas properly on the baking sheet and bake them once again for about 30 minutes.

Take them out and serve!

20. Marmite Smoothie

Smoothies are perfect for early morning breakfast as they keep you full for a longer period. This recipe of marmite smoothie is a unique twist or twirl in the regular smoothies which you have. This is going to be delicious as it is combined with peanut butter, bananas, Greek yogurt, and dates, wow! You have to try it, it is worth it!

Ingredients:

- 1 banana (ripened, sliced, frozen)
- 2 tbsp of Marmite
- Peanut butter (30 g)
- 1 tbsp of Greek yogurt
- 100 ml of milk
- 3 dates

Cooking Time - 5 minutes

Serving Size - 1

Instructions:

Take a blender and mix peanut butter, marmite, and banana. Blend them well.

Pour it in the serving glass and serve!

21. Marmite Roast Potatoes

Marmite roast potatoes are perfect snacks with enormous flavor and rich color. These roast potatoes are soft as well as fluffy from inside but crispy and crunchy from outside. If you are on a diet and can't eat anything tasty, this is going to be your solution in that case and you can try something new for your kids' snacks. This recipe is very easy to prepare as all you need is three ingredients: potatoes, cooking spray, and marmite. Just give it a try!

Ingredients:

- 4 potatoes (quarter-sized, boiled)
- 1 tbsp of Marmite
- Cooking spray

Cooking Time - 35 minutes

Serving Size - 4

Instructions:

Preheat the oven to 180°C.

Take a baking sheet and place all the pieces of potatoes.

Then, add the marmite, and coat them well with it. Spray some cooking oil on the potatoes.

Let them bake for 35 minutes.

Serve immediately!

22. Marmite Sprouts

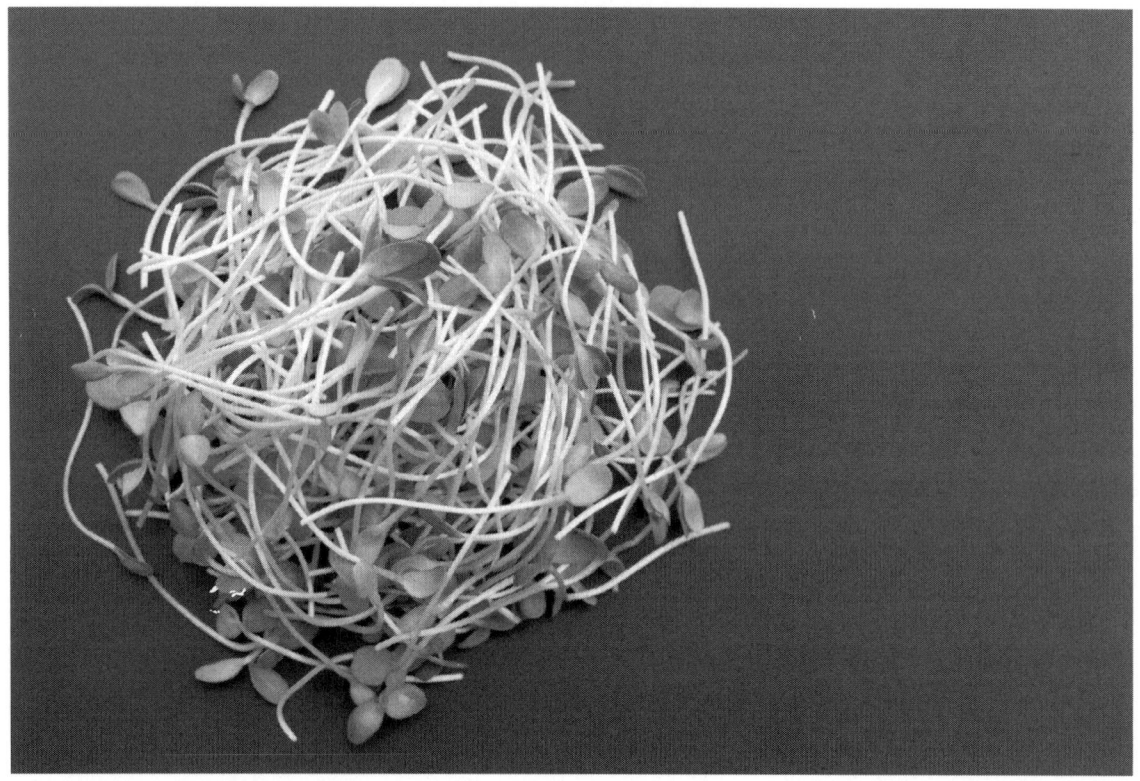

You might be thinking, sprouts and marmite together, what a weird combination! But do not worry at all, this recipe of marmite sprouts will not let you down. This recipe is quite tasty and easy to make and you will make it every next day. In this recipe, you will need only three ingredients as marmite, sprouts, and butter, and not only this but making them is not also difficult at all. This might be going to be your next favorite appetizer, so just give it a try.

Ingredients:

- 1/2 cup of butter (unsalted)
- 3 tsp of Marmite
- 2 cups of sprouts (halved)

Cooking Time - 10 minutes

Serving Size - 8

Instructions:

Take a bowl and mix butter with marmite, make a log with it on parchment paper, and form a Christmas cracker by rolling and then twisting it.

Let it chill for about a week.

Let the sprouts boil for about 5 minutes. Once they are done, let them dry.

Place a frypan over medium flame and add the boiled sprouts into it.

First, give them a dry fry for about 5 minutes.

Turn off the flame and add marmite and butter log, mix well.

Sprinkle it with the seasoning and serve!

23. Marmite Puff Pastry Pinwheel

This recipe of marmite puff pastry pinwheel is quite a unique and fun recipe to make. This might seem difficult to make but honestly, it is not, rather it is way easier than you can even think of. You just need three ingredients like puff pastry, cheddar cheese, and marmite. Apply marmite and cheddar cheese on the puff pastry and then bake them. This is all you need to do and your marmite puff pastry pinwheels are ready to be eaten within 15 minutes only!

Ingredients:

- 1 puff pastry roll
- 3/4 cup of cheddar cheese (grated)
- 3 tbsp of Marmite

Cooking Time - 15 minutes

Serving Size - 12

Instructions:

Preheat your oven to 220°C.

Apply a layer of marmite to the puff pastry roll with the help of a knife.

Now, add cheese over the layer of marmite.

Roll out the puff pastry from one end, it somewhat resembles a swiss roll.

Cut it into 2 cm slices.

Transfer all the slices to a baking tray and apply eggs into it.

Let them bake for about 20 minutes.

24. Marmite Cheesy Savoury Pudding

Marmite cheese savory pudding is a super delicious, luscious, flavorful, and completely amazing recipe that you can make for your lunch or dinner to make your family happy. All you need for this recipe is marmite, crumpets, eggs, milk, and cheddar cheese, you might think that it would be difficult to make but honestly, it is not. It is super easy so just try it once, you will surely fall in love with this one!

Ingredients:

- 2 crumpets
- 2 eggs
- 2 tbsp of Marmite
- 50ml of milk
- 1/2 cup of cheddar cheese

Cooking Time - 20 minutes

Serving Size - 1

Instructions:

Preheat the oven to 180°C.

Initially, roast the crumpets and apply a thin layer of marmite to them. Let them cut into two halves.

Grease a baking sheet and transfer the crumpets to the baking sheet.

Add half of the cheddar cheese in between each crumpet.

Now, mix the eggs well with the milk. Pour this mixture on the top of the crumpets.

Sprinkle the rest of the cheese on the top and place it in the oven.

Let it bake for about 15 minutes.

Serve hot!

25. Marmite Cashews

These marmite cashews are one of the most delicious party snacks you would ever find. These are full of flavor, crunchy, and crispy nuts to grab at any time you want. Prepare them whenever you want and the best part is that you can even store them in advance and that is for like two weeks in an air-tight container. You just need four ingredients for this like cashews, marmite, seasonings, and water. You can make them in just 12 minutes, isn't it great? Yeah, it is, so what are you waiting for? Just try them right away!

Ingredients:

- of cashew nuts (unsalted)
- 1 tsp. of Marmite
- 1 tsp of water
- Seasoning

Cooking Time - 12 minutes

Serving Size - 1

Instructions:

Preheat the oven at 200°C.

Take a frypan, place it over medium-low flame, and add water, cashews, marmite, and seasoning.

Coat the cashews well with the seasoning as well as marmite.

Now, transfer the cashews to a baking sheet and let them roast for 12 minutes.

Then, let them cool, and serve, or you may store them in an air-tight container.

26. Marmite Cheesy Stuffed Bloomer

This marmite cheese stuffed bloomer recipe is delicious and luscious that you won't stop eating it once you are done making it. This recipe can be made with just five ingredients like cheddar cheese, mozzarella cheese, marmite, white bloomer, and butter, so if you are a huge fan of cheese and marmite, then definitely this recipe is for you. And not only this, it is very easy to make filled with marmite and lots of cheese. You must give it a try right away!

Ingredients:

- 1-1/2 cups of white bloomer
- 3 tbsp of Marmite
- of butter
- of Cheddar (grated)
- of mozzarella (grated)

Cooking Time - 40 minutes

Serving Size - 1 loaf

Instructions:

Preheat the oven at 200°C.

Cut the loaf but make sure not to cut it all the way through.

Then, do the same thing just diagonally.

Mix butter with marmite in a pan placed over medium flame. Add cheddar and mozzarella cheese into the pan and mix them well.

Cover bread with the help of foil paper, keep it on the baking pan.

Let it bake for about 20 minutes.

Apply a layer of the butter mixture on it and then, again let it bake for 15 minutes.

Serve and enjoy!

27. Broccoli and Marmite Soup

Soup always does wonders if you have it on a cold winter night and what if we add an amazing flavor of marmite as well? Sounds delicious, right! This time, we will add an enormous favor to our broccoli soup and for sure, you are going to love this combination a lot. This recipe contains broccoli, potatoes, celery, vegetable stock, and marmite, of course. This is very easy to make, so just go for it and give it a try.

Ingredients:

- 1 tbsp of olive oil
- 2 cloves of garlic (chopped)
- 1 onion (chopped)
- 2 stalks of celery (sliced)
- 1 broccoli (chopped)
- 2 potatoes (peeled, diced)
- 1 tsp of marmite
- 500ml of vegetable stock
- Black pepper powder

Cooking Time - 30 minutes

Serving Size - 4

Instructions:

Gently heat the olive oil and fry the onions as well as celery a little bit.

Then, add chopped garlic into the pan and stir it well.

Now, add potatoes as well as broccoli into it, add some seasoning as black pepper powder.

Finally, add marmite and vegetable stock to it.

Let it boil and then lower the flame to simmer and cover it with the lid for about 20 minutes.

Blend it and make it smooth.

Serve!

28. Marmite French Onion Soup

Marmite French onion soup is a classic and authentic French recipe that is a perfect choice for these chilled nights, right! Here, a huge crouton filled with cheese, trying to impersonate as a soup that makes it way more soothing than you would ever think. Here, we have included one more amazing umami flavor of marmite with the various other flavors of bay leaves, white wine, onions, French baguette, cheddar cheese, and vegetable stock. This recipe is worth trying!

Ingredients:

- 4-3/8 cups of onions (halved)
- 2 tbsp of Olive oil
- 4 cloves of garlic (minced)
- 1 tbsp of Marmite
- 3 bay leaves
- 1 bottle of white wine
- 1 L. of vegetable stock
- 1 loaf of French baguette
- 1-1/4 cups of Cheddar (grated)
- 1 tbsp of pepper (grounded)

Cooking Time - 40 minutes

Serving Size - 6

Instructions:

Place a pan over medium flame and heat the olive oil. Brown the onions, garlic, bay leaves, and marmite.

Pour white wine and let the onions soak the wine.

Add the vegetable stock into it, let it simmer for about 30 minutes.

Pour it into the oven bowls. Add 2 pieces of the bread and top it with the cheese.

Grill it for about 10 minutes. Season it with black pepper powder.

Serve hot!

29. Marmite and Carrot Soup

Marmite and carrot soup bring quite a vibrant, bright, refreshing color due to the presence of carrots, lemon juice as well as ginger. The flavor enhances when we add marmite croutons into it, as it becomes a warm mixture of savory as well as sweet flavors. If you want, you can have this for lunch or you might have it for your dinner, it is just perfect any time. Try this recipe and you will fall in love with this.

Ingredients:

- 1/2 tsp of Marmite
- 4 slices of bread

For the Soup

- 1 tbsp of cooking oil
- 1 onion (sliced)
- 1 clove of garlic (crushed)
- 10 g of ginger (grated)
- 1/2 tsp of ginger (grounded)
- 2-1/4 cups of carrots (peeled, diced)
- 700 ml of vegetable stock
- Black pepper powder
- 1/2 tbsp of lemon juice

Cooking Time - 20 minutes

Serving Size - 2

Instructions:

Preheat the oven to 160°C.

Take a bowl and mix marmite with hot water.

Slice the bread into squares and then, pour marmite mixture over the pieces of the bread.

Grease a baking pan and keep the croutons over it. Let them bake for 20 minutes.

Now, heat oil into a saucepan and cook onions with ginger as well as garlic until they become tender.

Stir them for about a minute and then, add stock as well as carrots into it.

Let them boil for about 20 minutes.

Blend it well to make a fine paste and mix it with lemon juice.

Add black pepper powder and a little bit of salt into it according to your taste.

30. Tomato Soup and Marmite Toast

We cannot deny the fact that Tomato soup is a very common and an all-time favorite soup of everyone, right! It becomes even better when we add toast, soaked up into cheese flavor, then, nothing can compare to it. This recipe of tomato and marmite toast is filled with enormous flavor and works as a starter or a comforting food or supper. You can make this just within 15 minutes, and this makes this recipe even better!

Ingredients:

For the soup

- 1 tbsp of olive oil
- 1 onion (chopped)
- 1 tsp of oregano (dried)
- 1 clove of garlic (chopped)
- 1 bunch of basil leaves
- 1-1/2 cups of tomatoes

For the toast

- 2 slices of bread (toasted)
- 2 tsp of Marmite
- 1/2 cup of parmesan cheese (grated)

Cooking Time - 15 minutes

Serving Size - 2

Instructions:

Place the saucepan over medium flame and heat the oil, add onions, salt, and stir for about 5 minutes.

Then, add garlic, basil, and oregano. Cook for about a minute initially, and then, reduce the flame to simmer for about 10 minutes.

Blend it with the help of a hand blender and add black pepper powder to it.

Let the grill heat high and toast the bread with marmite on it. Then, apply a layer of parmesan over it.

Keep the slices of bread on the baking pan and let them grill for about 5 minutes.

Pour the soup into two bowls, top it with marmite toast and parmesan cheese.

Season it with black pepper powder. Serve it.

Conclusion

So, here you have it all in the end. I hope you had a great time reading this Marmite cookbook. You must have noticed that all the recipes mentioned above are quite easy to follow and this makes it possible to prepare these dishes and enjoy your food. It is your call now, prepare a variety of scrumptious food for all your friends as well as family members and astonish them with your amazing cooking skills.

So, fasten your apron, get ready with all the kitchen equipment and ingredients you need, and set your favorite movie or TV series on your television screens, as it is the time to eat delicious and luscious Marmite recipes. So, what are you waiting for? Go, your kitchen is waiting for you. Make these palatable dishes right away. You may also experiment by using some other ingredients and discover some of your new recipes.

HAPPY COOKING!

Author's Afterthoughts

I would like to express my deepest thanks to you, the reader, for making this investment in one my books. I cherish the thought of bringing the love of cooking into your home.

With so much choice out there, I am grateful you decided to Purch this book and read it from beginning to end.

Please let me know by submitting an Amazon review if you enjoyed this book and found it contained valuable information to help you in your culinary endeavors. Please take a few minutes to express your opinion freely and honestly. This will help others make an informed decision on purchasing and provide me with valuable feedback.

Thank you for taking the time to review!

Christina Tosch

About the Author

Christina Tosch is a successful chef and renowned cookbook author from Long Grove, Illinois. She majored in Liberal Arts at Trinity International University and decided to pursue her passion of cooking when she applied to the world renowned Le Cordon Bleu culinary school in Paris, France. The school was lucky to recognize the immense talent of this chef and she excelled in her courses, particularly Haute Cuisine. This skill was recognized and rewarded by several highly regarded Chicago restaurants, where she was offered the prestigious position of head chef.

Christina and her family live in a spacious home in the Chicago area and she loves to grow her own vegetables and herbs in the garden she lovingly cultivates on her sprawling estate. Her and her husband have two beautiful children, 3 cats, 2 dogs and a parakeet they call Jasper. When Christina is not hard at work creating beautiful meals for Chicago's elite, she is hard at work writing engaging e-books of which she has sold over 1500.

Make sure to keep an eye out for her latest books that offer helpful tips, clear instructions and witty anecdotes that will bring a smile to your face as you read!

Printed in Great Britain
by Amazon

35270609R00046